Slaugh

Sundress Publications • Knoxville, TN

Editor: Erin Elizabeth Smith
Editorial Assistant: Kanika Lawton
Editorial Interns: Eliza Browning, Abigail Renner, Claire Shang

Colophon: This book is set in Bell MT.

Cover Image: "Salvaged Feathers" by Olivia Joy St. Claire

Cover Design: Kristen Ton

Author Photo: Ryley Eden Priest

Book Design: Erin Elizabeth Smith

Slaughter the One Bird
Kimberly Ann Priest

Acknowledgements

The 3288 Review: "Strawberry Picking," "Trailer House," "Wind Chime"

Anti-Heroin Chic: "A Reflection on Pathos"

ArLiJo: "My Friend Believes She Wishes a Miscarriage Into Reality,"
"Sunday Morning"

The Berkeley Poetry Review & as the winner of the 2019 Heartland Poetry
Prize in *New Poetry from the Midwest* anthology by *New American
Press*: "Practice"

The Coachella Review: "They Cling"

The Comstock Review: "Husk"

Glass: A Journal of Poetry: "my pedophile stays in the moment"

The Meadow: "This is Not My First Flat Earth Poem," "She," "Everything
Left Open," "Preparing the Body"

Mothers Always Write: "Husbandry"

New Delta Review: "my pedophile is obsessed with details," "my pedophile
requires attention"

Nightingale and Sparrow Press: "After Molested, the Child Remembers
Nothing," "The Scream," "my pedophile prefers my childhood"

The Sierra Nevada Review: "my pedophile suddenly turns me on," "my
pedophile times all my future orgasms," "my pedophile experiences
superficial pleasure," "my pedophile takes me into his confidence,"
"my pedophile has a discerning palette"

Stormcellar: "Theodicy"

Thimbleletter: "Intimate Things"

Welter: "my pedophile produces a cinematic frame"

Windhover & as a contest winner for *Women Under Scrutiny: The
(Dis)Comfort) of Our Bodies, Ourselves* anthology from *Brooklyn Girl
Books*: "Record of Wrongs"

Contents

// the house //

EX POST FACTO

//. . . but now sin, where that reigns in a house, is a plague there, as it is in a heart. Masters of families should be aware, and afraid of the first appearance of sin in their families, and put it away, whatever it is.

. . . the infected part must be taken out. If it remains in the house, the whole must be pulled down. The owner had better be without a dwelling, than live in one that was infected

. . . sin ruins families and churches. Thus sin is so interwoven with the human body that it must be taken down by death. //

Matthew Henry, Commentary on Leviticus 14:33-53

// Open closed open. That's all we are. //

Yehuda Amichai

// Theodicy

In the photograph, I am four years old
wearing my father's navy cap,
posing atop a mattress: blue and white striped coverlet
to match my white t-shirt and cobalt pants.
I look every bit Popeye—blond pigtails, fists at my waist.
My father bends his arms—gangly as mine—to take
the photograph.

I wonder now if this is the bed,
if this is the coverlet
on which my legs were spread the width of a hand,
on which the optical system of my eyes collected
dimly lit contours of a man's face—
the every-other-Sunday gaze
of a pedophile, third seat, first row, next to
the pastor's wife,
smiling like the broken swag of moon draped across
my bedroom floor, passage to the closet,
burrow, bed, one finger-width crack between closet doors,
my labia safely gathered in a hand—

waiting to leave this space the morning after
my mother finds underwear crumpled beneath a chest
of drawers, and me in the closet remembering nothing.

Thirty years later, remembering something:
this space, sheets bunched and threaded through our limbs,
my husband's silent-smiling face, a door
safely gathered in his hand,
one finger width-crack of vagina—burrow, bed, third seat,

first row of the moon, me
collecting the eyes of my father when he says he didn't know
he had left me with a pedophile—
the contours of my marriage spread the mere depth
of a photograph.

1.

// . . . take two birds . . . // Leviticus 14:49

Midwestern Doe Story

In the wood, the doe has located paths—carcass damp—
and kissed the still-warm broken cobs,

nibbled tracks struggling forward, romancing the road
where she, feasting,

blames the slow skate of hooves on pavement—thin legs,
late harvest and absence of green,

her lack of youth, an early fetus—and steps
into a cavern of light.

Her lungs tight with cold as she lunges toward the ditch
opposite but,

live kick of tires on ice, sharp pang—stunning, cinematic,
bright. The shock of it all

skidding toward an out-take,
fucked-up windshield and running board steam.

The driver hobbling, looking for his optics,
and bounding from his seat—

thankful it is only the animal dying. Maybe some pieces
could be salvaged for meat.

Trailer House

My son reaches for my sympathy, constantly.
He wants more of me—
this boy nearly grown into a man wants more.

I could tell him that when he was merely a button
stitched to the lining of my coat,
a bead tucked into my shell, a kernel of wheat
starring itself to an ovular wound in my earth,

I shook,

carried my body to the floor, held it there,
felt his fetus ingesting—my day-to-day existence
pre-packaged and fertilized in a 14x70 trailer house;

I was windowed, the trailer door knocked loose,
knob spilling with universe,
boundaries tampered with, renamed:
the way my husband never hit me but always left a bruise.

Now that my husband is gone,
the windowpanes indulge the sky,
and my son stands in the kitchen daring me to flee—
light shoved into his eyes like broken crystal.

He can't see the organic parts of me stitched, tucked,
starred—the wound of his father suckling
a monster already grown,
consuming all my sympathy.

I adjust the curtain,
fill the sink with water and soap, grab a dish, apply
a sponge, pull ever so gently away.

After Molested, the Child Remembers Nothing

1985

She squirms in the belly of a rowboat
clutching the reel of a fishing rod
in her left hand
and reaches toward a can of worms
with the other

anxious to spear them,
watch their fat bodies wriggle,
ripples circling prey.

Later, her father slices the caught fish open,
sometimes proclaiming *It's a female!*
while pulling out a white sack
of eggs,

milky bubbles housing
tiny black dots, eyes that ogle
the insides—a worm clinging to the ovaries,
slipping through their slimy gaze.

Everything Left Open

The ball joint of a showerhead wrenched into place,
wisht of water sputtering its cup, so easy
to tease into exertion.

Outside the window, bats in the alleyway
and underneath the eaves
rejoin this world—my husband's silent sweat at 1AM: pine,
nicotine, gasoline, toothpaste.

My bare chest pressed against the plastic brightening
with scum,
his cum draining out of me like fire ants
into a porthole where their red bellies will smooth out
a labyrinth of veins,
pant of buzzards circling a doe's pronged cavern
carved open by running board and wheel,

all his camshafts humming,
black smudges on a marker board that no one can erase,

the dozen or more times I told him this was not the way into
a woman's body
but he couldn't hear me over his mother's voice
begging a newspaperman on the phone
to please never print the story about alcohol, minors,
and his car.

He was seventeen.
I was casualty waiting to happen.

Just a little less obvious than the apartment house behind us:
A man stumbling up the stairway, drops a bottle between steps.
A woman locks the door.
He kneels among the flowerpots searching for a key.

The mirror in our bathroom discloses everything left open.
I search for a towel,
make sure my husband is asleep.

Turtle Doves

You have caged a pair of turtledoves
in our bedroom—

cliché for protecting the innocent,

rubbing their bellies through bars and mimicking
their coos.

They pull into question marks,

and huddle nearer
each other,

resisting your reach.

Still,   you touch them:

man and wife.   Coo, coo.

Anything worth having requires

sacrifice.

Strawberry Picking

I like the feel of a strawberry at the moment it is plucked
from the vine, the weighted cup of my hand,
the delicately applied pressure of two fingers and thumb,
the pull. My bucket is yellow. My headscarf paisley
taupe and white. I cradle the berry's polished flesh
and lift it to my lips to suckle its tear dropped onto
my tongue, exploding with seed and red. My son
watches me, a row of vines between us, his small face
rounding over the berry in my teeth as he plucks
a berry from his bucket, bites hard, the nipple broken,
bleeding down his cheek. He smiles. I smile
and hold half a berry in my hand. He lifts a smashed stem.
We are marooned in rows and rows of vine and leaves,
licking our lips. I reach over the tangle between us
and give my son the half-berry. He matches my reach,
pinching the stem between two fingers and thumb
and pulls the berry gently to suckle its juice, while closing
his eyes and lifting his face to the afternoon sun.

A Study of *Woman with Peacock,* Center Panel, of *The Garden of Earthly Delights*

Naked figures seek pleasure in various ways,
says the Wikipedia inscription—

but does not mention that the figures are all women
or that various assumes the presence of bright birds and fruit;

does not consider assumptions surrounding seduction.

Does not name the type of fruit—strawberries
dancing above the heads of the pale ample-bottomed women,
or the dark woman holding a round red berry up for inspection
in her charcoal hand.

Does not assume that the viewer is so easily a sinner,
readily seduced;

or that this naked trinity is just as much infancy as mature sexuality
and as I see it

Bosch, presiding over delight, is uncomfortable with both—

how portraits of supposed innocence are so vulnerable and,
paradoxically, soliciting response.

Does not realize how much I love fruit

or that, here, in Michigan, the gardens make summer a paradise
and my children and I have walked rows
of various produce, filling our buckets
and feasting.

That everything is fleshed.
That flesh is not deadly,

and I, being woman, bursting with color and flight, am enjoying
my paradise
in no particularly womanlike way,

spinning the syllables of my body against a fertile landscape
and burying my knuckles
deep into the painter's ample-esurient lips.

They Cling

Wingspan for shouldering witness,
things seen but

weighted with inflection—flicker
of light on wide teeth.

Synonyms split like fireflies in glass—
surveyed, examined.

Moths collide
with all eyes open—too minuscule to see

the screen door's wire cage. A pair
of scissors:

heavy are my hands.
Your mouth cut like a newspaper clipping—

brief confirmation of a face
humming like a dial tone, a very clear

connection; the way
he also hummed from ear lobe to artery

to waist—
to the pale skin circumferencing

my labia where the hair is shaved
and the follicles

have never seen the light. I see
the light licking at our roof beams,

its energy worn out
rehearsing re-entry, repeating

do this in remembrance of he. I do.
You wipe

your penis clean with the shirt, discarded,
at the end of our bed

as though the half-hard limb
in your hand is object, sharp, ready to

be sheathed.
And you face me as you do this,

taking in the whole scene:
My under-spread body pried open

enough, slightly.
Your flipped-up finger

already cleansed of any afterthoughts
of me, lukewarm and leaving

the slaughter re-composing
the first time a pedophile carved up

my seams.
I lie in the heart of the afterglow, naked,

both men bisecting
this bomb-shelter night.

// EX POST FACTO:
A Body Memory

Maybe it is

the cut of his eyes—

               the room
      closes like a closet, slips into his body
                     hoping for a door.
She feels her way across
        currents
            surging,
                 heaving.

Walls
crash, water
breaks—

        He fishes tears out of the torrent, says
because you were molested

               to her mouth.

2.

// . . .slaughter the one bird. . . // Leviticus 14:50

Sunday Morning

1985

A girl in the third row counts the seconds it would take
for a man twice her age to undress her.

There are many ways to find God, says the preacher:
inside a belly, inside a cave,

inside the spirit of a man.
Her mother sits on a long hard pew underlining verses,

deep creases in her forehead and the corners of her eyes.
The young man, tranquil

next to the preacher's wife,
turns again to see the girl with his deep brown eyes.

The preacher holds his Bible open like a plate over-filled
at a picnic.

The girl learns the hungry are filled if they are seeking—
the girl learns to keep her gaze straight ahead.

The pastor's wife smiles at the man in the front row
and he smiles back.

Her mother is marking each minute with *Amen.*
There is only one way to know God, says the preacher,

from outside the brothels, from outside the bars,
from outside, the Spirit will come.

She

is reborn of secrets and teeth—
two thighs crafted in anguish
and fitted to her pelvis
as though they have no home.
All air and water.
All tears and blood.
Outside her window,
two birds cow as night turns
to morning, wedding its black bonnet
to the backside of the moon;
her infant hands choose four feathers
from their phantom screams
covering her ears, sinking
their needles
deep into the pores behind her lobes
like a panacea—
bones fluting with
trajectories, admonitions, arteries,
and scenes from an afterlife
she waits long and lonely to believe.
Dropping light around her body,
she hopes she will be
counted with the righteous despite
the invisible strings
tied around her bones, tugging,
dancing her slowly
toward the judgement of the sun's
bold, impassive face.

Soft Fruit

Is it you? Are you there,
thief I can't see . . .

-Kathleen Fraser, "Poem Wondering if I am Pregnant"

A poorly lit corridor of snow
      opens the forest,

shocked with pine needles, saplings,
      and grey,

the frozen pond
      pregnant with reflection,

and the moon, a bullet hole
      in its icy pane.

A doe steps into its solstice, her bones
      undressing for the season,

growing desire to give up a life:
      river in rib, soft fruit

caught between two leaves, branch
      in the fire of her belly

breaking. And though
      the air is silent—no explosion,

bird call or breeze—she lifts
      her ears. Swiftly,

they fly—footprints on the path
      speaking only of she.

Preparing the Body

Wash your fingers of oil in skin,
straighten and thrust to blemish the inside of her shell—

the calcite of which shatters, the animal within
already rotted.

Say this is your sympathy, allowing a chamber,
arrowing the inside of her cup

then show her the shell—
how it is polished on the outside, but this is not enough.
How each laceration uncovers its luster.

Say *Do not flinch so expressively—the cut is not for killing, but
for keeping,*

while setting wire fingers on the table next to
a cold scoop of visceral mass.   Be omniscient, but

share the dial of a microscope. Examine the animal

together.

*

Together,
the moment will be carved into ten thousand groans,
an assembly of converts tossing their hair to the rhythm

of chiseled stone—

gridlocked, gasping,
         demanding a portion of whatever is left.
Two limbs so cheap on this market,

                but four—
       now that is worth consideration.

Want her for only twenty seconds,   then nothing.

Make sure she knows she can't eat too little
or crave too much to make a difference—
the price is always the same because

the ones that go the quickest and for the highest price   are not
the ones who make themselves ready,
      but the ones who need attention the most.

Like worshippers, they have appetites—

            led along by just a tiny minnow
            dangled from a stick.

      *

     And when he tells her to gird up her loins
       —by which she thinks he means the body is not
        her home—

he says there is no explicit connection between his verbs
        and his hands.

He learned this in church.

She learned
and

wants to be the hero of this story
for at least this would exonerate her doubts

        but she is not incorporeal: his verbs are like
her hands.

          *

        Open your mouth, he says—be kind.

Husbandry

Our son was only a year old
when you told him

divorce is the worst thing
that could happen to a family

then went outside
to water fruit trees.

A breeze curled the kitchen curtain
against its window frame.

Our son drank all the apple juice
in his sippy cup.

I prayed *Lord, Lord,*
give me a sign

and watched you through
the window,

sunlight playing with
your shirt—my belly ripe against

the countertop,
our daughter kicking inside.

Holy Ground

It is not
the thought of a man
I question,
but the smell of him
the sight of him,
the feel of his thumb
caressing the back
of my neck—
because it all seems
too honest,
far too much
I am that I am: a phrase
slithering around
my bones,
matriarching
my creases and folds,
mocking me
for craving its audacity,
wanting to put it
in my mouth
and savor its juice—
to speak it back pointing
at the rod of a man's
power,
to command
throw it down
and watch the rod
lasso up into
a spineless noose.
My husband's people—

male after male
after male—groaning
under the weight
of tyranny,
dependent on
his bravery
to release them,
cleanse them of fear.

A Reflection on Pathos

Rabbits circle near the raspberry bushes searching
for something to eat.

My son reaches to brush his baby fingers
over their backs and ears—

they freeze, startle, escape,
the grass waving behind them like a soft crop

of hair,
a landscape so unmolested—perfect.

Some say he looks like his father. I think
he looks like me, every mite and particle; his

thick brows and bold jaw demanding
attention, but not the sort that most sons do.

I taught him to be mine, to remember
the consequence of matriphagy, how Eve

guided mothers toward the importance of sons—
to let them consume,

protect their fragile egos after ritual offering. And how
this pathos favors touch.

Silence in our most holy texts replaced with,
and he went to her and comforted her.

Coping. Sex.
Cain begotten in a shed behind the house

where the tools for gardening are kept. *When not
in paradise*, reads the sign above the door—an unfinished

phrase. If only we knew beforehand
what would come of our longings

for Eden. What damage we would make.
My son, a shadow of some image stumbling

away from me. I pull his infant body to my body, cut
his waist into my hip, point toward

the bushes. He follows my reach with his eyes,
observes the rabbits searching for insects

in the grass. Against what we know of their nature,
today they are craving fresh meat.

Practice

Autumn. Leaves drip and turn over,
round like the goblet of a thigh torn from its animal.

Daylight folds into creases,
a jumbled marathon of birds strung loosely along
telephone wires
and my hair canvasing light paned across the bed's
worn coverlet.

By dusk I will have imagined that dirt roads
are highways
and the cold steel beams of our trailer
are thick layers of shadow from oaks
pressed into aluminum beating out the doormats
caked with mud.

Rifle fire in the distance.

The first signs of winter. Your boots
dragging the teeth of rotten corn across this barren field.

        If I let you nuzzle me,
        will you leave the children alone?

Your hands shake. Bullets clip trees.

I hear them through these thin paper panels
that tremble with your knuckle prints: each near miss,
my cheekbones
flush as a newly-skinned hide.

Target panic is a condition caused by trying too hard to hit your mark;
it can only be cured by a closer range.

Once you met a doe on the path near our home.
You said she didn't move, she wanted you to touch her.

The Scream

/ / a body memory / /

Fingers flay the spine—tentacles rising from a slit
        of vagina

undressing nerves in her torso, shoulders, breasts—
her whole frontal lobe
live-wired, eight-years-old.

He flew her out like a hundred dove-pieces homing,
their domestic cries sharpened by the whirlwind reaped
when no one was looking—

        a pulpy lace thing stirring with her cervix.

She screamed—not aloud—when he helped her off the bed,
led her body to the door.

// EX POST FACTO:
How They Bond

She asks him to

let go,

       he smiles, sways

       a little like a mother with
       a child,

says *calm down, it's*

           okay,

holds her chin firmly to his chest,

hugs
      her shoulders tighter.

       I will, he answers,
       if you can stay controlled.

// the house //

my pedophile is obsessed with details

when he says appropriate / he is not referring to the
number of dollies in the room or how well they are
centered on the tables or whether or not the items on
the dollies are centered on the dollies or the
arrangement of the room is equal to the arrangement of
dollies so that the dollies themselves do not attract all
of the attention in the space / he is referring to whether
or not they are essential to the space since the rooms
should not be a composition of dollies // as in // some
attention should be given to the frame of things // for
instance // the fact that all the items in the room are
less than the room / the windows // the plaster // the
paint // the hard wood floors // the doorways // the
beams beneath / above / behind everything // these
things / he says / are essential having nothing to do
with my hands or my feet or how they are connected to
my body / or how he wants the right to space
everything symmetrically / rearrange a life in the most
appropriate way

my pedophile requires attention

when he speaks of proximity / he is not referring to the
fading photograph in the hall or the razor blade rusting
in the shower or the silver frame on the dressing table
for which there is no glass / he is speaking of making
things / dried glue peeling on his fingertips / sequins
and glitter in small drinking cups, plastic membranes of
synthetic roses // smell of polish remover and paint //
the sickly slice in his thumb from an X-Acto knife / the
cut he keeps opening and closing like a lipless pair of
lips / the popsicle stick shoved under his mouth playing
patient to the doctor of his hand / the "O" he says while
thinking an "Ah" / the runway out his doorway littered
with bright colored feathers // sparkles // and things

my pedophile seeks a cozier space

if he says we are safe / it is the long sloped surface of a
bath towel woven with innumerable loops and folded
around the small of his back / the button of his waist /
resting on the cap of each knee / how it is acceptable
attire in the morning / the bathroom mirror portraiting
his robe // white shaving cream // white toothpaste //
white smile // white from waistline to knees // all the
color of the room reflected in his skin tone / visible only
to thin razors scoring the escarpment of his cheek /
lifting and cutting away / how if he says we are not safe
/ he does not refer to the steam fogging up the shower
due to a dysfunctional fan or how everything is too
moist and the razor keeps slipping and the towel leaves
his body too wet / no / he is referring to the towels in
the closet and how they were not folded in thirds but
were folded in halves / overextending the limits of their
allowable girth

my pedophile celebrates his limbs

if he is satisfied it is portrait by number / half-moon of pink spooning ocular greens / papyri corridors // ganglionic walls // a hemic marketplace creasing the stairway // the button of his choosing fitted with infinitesimal mouths poised to call back curtains of chrysalis and wing / butterfly houses for sale on the road to embargo / his elbow in the mouth of a wasp nest // all honey, no sting // insert one pin into the hair on a brown beetle's back and it will tell you he is fortunate to have all his pinchers free in their sockets // half-moon of bone spooning ocular tweeze as he sets all the silver pinheads in a cushion only to pull them one little limb at a time

my pedophile is performance ready

he reshapes the face of the clock / bends its left arm forward enough to greet a neighbor but backward enough to laugh at the small dimple in his chin and brushes the number 9 off of its cheek before its right arm knows that his two legs are saddling the 7 / a whole room of people going for a ride / silly and balancing the 8 over his nose // everyone thinking he is silly // the children too // the 0 in 10 sucking in its sides to impress his audience as he squeezes his hand around the 6 / reaches for a 5 / changes his mind / asks for a 4 / drinks soda water out of a cup // the 3 taking a deep breath / noticing the outline of the 1

my pedophile produces a cinematic frame

if it is pornographic / there is the soft spread of butter
on toast / the few crumbs that suck salt from its yellow-
white solid / thick with table knife scraping the center
into furrows / yellow running onto white plate showing
through deep cuts / and if she is nude the eggs are
undercooked / soft round bulb of yellow shaped bright
bulb / fork impressions on transparent shield / the full
runny width of white plate / and if there is sex it is
embryo // salt // slices of toast / but if it is breakfast /
it is me // the whole white surface // bright and
bulbing //undercooked // tight as egg // how much he
loves salt / to lick it from the surface / butter rolled
over his tongue / the way he sets the knife at the edge
of the plate after preening yellow yolk from its teeth and
never talks about porn or nudity or sex yet I feel
photographed / a film played across a makeshift screen
/ white sheet // clothespins // the cheap re-enactment
of something he eats // the eggs // the toast // the
butter of me spread over its surface

my pedophile takes me into his confidence

pouring is equal to panting if the wine glass he is
holding cannot decide how long it will stand at the
windowsill and study the view / if rolling two words
together is merely to steady their sounds / if when
closing one eye he patches the other with a short e and
reaches through the wire screen to grab loose
advertisements falling from the sky while all the other
party goers act ambivalent / if confetti / if he has just
passed me a drink as though it is a corpse / if under the
bed someone is listening and it's not he or me or anyone
we know

my pedophile times all my future orgasms

if he says we have time it is the shape of the glass / how it is blown with air / how the glassblower covers its mouth and handles its bulb / how light is a word for knowledge // weight // and touch / how all are invisible / and if I believe it is time it is the bubble / the oxygenated seed that rises to the surface im-perfecting the whole shape // a welt // a blemish // a seam / but if he tells me it is not time / then table salt sifts slowly through the slender neck of the hourglass turned over // then over // then over again / whispering / relenting

my pedophile remains objective

he washes his hands / smooths a freckle of glass //
burn-marks where the dishwater caught fire //
discovers the strength of acetylene every time he holds
a clean finger up to a mirror / this is where the smoke
becomes insightful / full of dancing matches no one will
ever get to light / he lights them to illuminate
watermarks on knives // spoons // a fork / so well-
pronged / standing upright in a cup / holding its figure
just so / as though it is a finger // a match // or pillar
of smoke / his tongue wicks too close to its flame / he
stands upright / places his eyes on two platters /
immerses them in dishwater // white frothy bubbles /
small pieces of leftover meat

my pedophile prefers my childhood

if he is not satisfied / it is the shift of dry beans between
paper plates // a bubble exploding too softly // that
silicon wheeze a soda cap makes when only asking
simple questions: what sort of woman likes flannel //
sharp pencils // and strawberry lemonade / the form of
the question being merely symbolic / not attempting to
gain information or trust / chimes on the front door //
pool in the backyard // the grass strewn with toys too
wet now to touch / dolls in the house shaped like real
Barbies / but hollow // shorter // not weighing
enough / less easy to pose in a tiny Barbie kitchen /
plopped on a mattress / a carpet / a couch fainting with
love

my pedophile suddenly turns me on

as fidget is to form or the fragment of a flower pressed
into a book that no one ever reads / he sits like a pipe
// smoke-stack // memory of a time when boyish is a
thing / page after page after page reading for new
storylines // bored // busy with the handle on the toilet
tank / with injury // satire // and flank // with my
head coddling the melody of saxophones // cymbals //
and strings / a flickering TV / what soap is to opera /
what stamina means when it's paired up with pray /
what the remote tells him is ready for viewing when he
holds it up to the light / caresses the buttons / feels the
fat one near the top and lifts it toward the screen

EX POST FACTO

// This is Not My First Flat Earth Poem

// with lines from Psalm 33 //

My body is being a body again

taking photos of itself in the bathroom where the windows
don't facilitate too much light—glass

blocks stacked like bricks. Like

bricks, my body is wielding its bones at the damaged mirror, smoky
under a low hanging light,
where the waters of the sea are gathered like a heap

and I mouth a protest concerning
the shape of a thing I cannot command: the plans of a man's heart.
I hold

my purse close to my hip, and my hip
holds my questions close to me—the image reflected
one-dimensional, resisting their every curve and dot. But

by its great might
[the image] cannot rescue

me from asking. I cavort the landscape as if I possess
a pair of wandering eyes

and could tease out the same answers a viewer might awake
standing before "The Garden of Earthly Delights"

at the Museo Nacional Del Prado,
its panels closed concealing the historically unknowable inside.

Like still life, not landscape, Bosch

has painted the world flat inside a bubble, and fed it
with springs, a biblical mist

mounting hills, cushioning the trees so that their porous trunks
are fleshed ever so softly.

        Softly,
the round bulb dips its buttocks into the open air of this tiny
bathroom,
safely exposed,
too hot to touch—
and the bathroom walls remember they are peeling.
Outside its doors, Shakey Graves suggests that the bartenders
and drinkers try to forget all them enemies and debts.
Of course, the tabs go up,

the laughter, the music. Fists
in pockets. Bar brawls are rare—or so I've observed.

        I keep myself useful
          to the scenery:

lip gloss instead of red lips. Jeans. A rain jacket in case. No tequila
or whiskey.

I am as poetic as one bottle of Corona Light.

Finished with my drink, I slipped into this space, shed

my energy, rearrange the hair around my face.

       Dear Mirror,

       if we are discussing the clouds that rub their breasts
       against the bald dome of the earth's protective sphere
       then we might as well admit, the beginning
       of everything is always a little sexy:

a stranger pays for my beer like a friend.

After that, the music begins to feel like the Lord is looking down
from the heaven,
his back arched and the whole damn creation
supine;

from a learned distance I watch the panels begin to open
and know he will see what he thinks he has made,
how it is so

               explorable, over and around—

how it can be opened.
How it can be closed.

How it can be
opened again.

Its unlatched cover spread across a surface—peek-a-boo,
there you are—

               all the tempting children of men.

3.

// . . . take . . . the live bird, and dip [it] in the
blood of the slain bird . . . cleanse the house with the
blood of the [slain] bird . . . // Leviticus 14: 51, 52

Wind Chime

At the screen door, she listens to the driftwood chips
threaded with cord, hanging from the rafters

of their porch—tick, tick. Her husband
enters her mind like a needle of light through clouds:

The sky is large here, he says, so she looks up,
a sliver of orange peeling over the horizon,

as a broken moon cuts through its enlarging darkness.
Thunder peels. Rain applauds against the cement stoop,

then reaches one invisible hand
through the screen door's latch to wrestle it loose.

She lets the wind play god as silos rumble
like timpani drums in the distance, lightning pulsing

black, then white. *If you ever leave me,*
her husband once told her, *I'll take everything:*

your home, your children, your mind.
She still has all three: a wind chime always shifts,

never breaks. One summer,
she found it splayed across the porch floor after a rainstorm,

the cord frayed so badly it had to be replaced.
She rethreaded the chips, left them to dry in the sun.

Six Does Kiss the Fields

The smell of onions and garlic through a window,
dark birth of three million stars, late into the whisper
of fog and a neighbor's TV, six does kiss the field
beside the trailer, their yearlings close behind.
Desperate lick of salt, an open palm, rustling leaves against
a partly damaged shed. Men roam the woods
as though gifted with gestation, their eyes, stories
as tearless as the nights they choose to wander beneath
a Hunter's Moon—waxing, waning, full—maybe
ripped open by bullet or blade. The umber trees wielding
too many bodies to crows: not enough huntsmen
skilled in their craft. Hair and fresh meat left
on running boards, tires that barrel carelessly away.
Months of anticipation and the urge to fill one's arms
with warm flesh. A doe predicting which young
survive 'til spring, when she'll ripen again, if she's lucky—
all of her warriors struck down in the fields.

Intimate Things

Penitent hinge that reassures
            a door,
private corner of a lover's lips,
two palms facing each other to steeple—

        these things to say, this is duty.

Worn crease of an envelope,
letters I write to you in the shower aware now
            I do have that coveted space
            between my thighs,
            warm lemon drops—

        these things to say I take some pleasure
        in this.

The clasp on my grandmother's locket
            spilling from its velvet casing
            onto the bedroom floor—

        this to say your attention is expected.

I can pick it with my thumbnail:
            open, open, close.

My Friend Believes She Wishes a Miscarriage Into Reality

It dropped out of me
bloody.   I mean
it was bloody in the bathroom—I stood
in a pool of blood—   No,
sat in it—   No,   laid in my bed. No,   cried. No,
—I didn't.

I was bleeding
not in the bathroom
not in my bed   but

in the shop while working earlier that morning,
cutting foam and stems, filling vase after vase with water,
arranging flowers for a wedding, and singing
"Dani California"—   singing—
sweating out pink drops, dropping
a leaf, a petal, a card: congratulations on your special day,
the fetus.

Did I tell you I was singing?

        I was.

I didn't tell you I wanted the child.
I didn't tell anyone
or buy a plastic stick to know if it was even there.
The sloppy mass was on the bathroom floor.

I mopped it up, dried myself, slept
the whole next day.

Husk

/ / a contrapuntal / /

whisper soft into the ear of   my friend
corn growing   out of time
out of season   in the barren field
in the barren womb   of a mother
—a stalk   green
dismembered   broke open
laying on the earth   spilled
too many white pearls   counted
pursed between   her lips
quivering feathers of   flesh
silk   like bowstrings
flossing a breeze   teeth
sallow   scattered
pockets of silence—   sown
sweet corn   never
plucked   never kissed clean

Record of Wrongs

You get used to the mouth as a funnel,
loaded muzzle of a gun close-range, cocked,
waiting to go off the moment you shove
a finger down your throat.

Bitch, my husband said, not tired of counting every sin
I committed at 3AM when I peeled my body out of bed
and tiptoed to the kitchen
for a sliver of chicken pressed onto a Wheat Thin,

because I'd eaten almost nothing all day,
nothing I kept in my stomach,
the lean minutes that crawled the walls of our trailer
starved for some warm animal

to hug its floorboards praying *forgive us*
for we know not what we do.
If only the cupboards were not full of blanks
gaping with evidence that I had my mother's disease:

a bag of chips on her thighs, collapsing
one by one by one. I watched her and said
I'd never do this, be that way, the devils gloating
when they caught me descending the stairs, fifteen,

my father sizing me up, then asking my mother,
why can't you be skinny like this?
It's not that my husband meant the same when he said
he was glad I am small because he is small

and—for his manhood—this is a very good thing.
And it isn't that he wanted me to feel bad
about bulimia; it's just that he wanted me to know
he knows I do this.

Not like the cigarette he lit five miles from home,
smoking out the window of his car
so the scent wouldn't settle in the seats,
then flung it out into the darkness along the dirt road

while his headlights poked holes through our kitchen
where I washed dishes
aware he would enter smelling
of fresh cologne and nicotine;

but I didn't say a word because this too
would be counted against me as keeping a record of wrongs—
no greater sin, he claimed, forgiving me
completely—confiscating all my ammunition.

A Body Memory

Screen doors excusing the house
for its permanence,
hand puppet of a child in the hall. I think I know her name,
but cannot remember.

When she wakes me, this morning, asking for a ride to school
I freeze,

anxiously caught
in a metaphor, the pen now recalling
the page,

telling the story for me—

how it feels like something my body remembers, but after
I've written it down
I realize

I am drunk:

opiates and cortisone—the tonic pleasure
of releasing

no energy, no language—no force for force, only
drip—drip—drip—drip,

the scent of my ex-husband clawing basal ganglia,

how it feels to run my finger over his ear, slip my tongue between
his teeth,

the pleasure of

force—force, drip—drip.

Untouched

I drag an ice cube over my tongue
and eye you from the bed
as you knot your tie for work, rinse
pomade into your hair—so clean,
so middle-class
You didn't hit me last night.
You never do.
You never sweat a thin sheen of booze
and Nautica Blue,
swilling among the sheets,
200-count cotton/polyester blend
handed down from your mother.
You never ask me for a glass
of whiskey, shaky,
eager to take a pinch
out of my thigh.
You never complain about the chilled
linoleum floor
in the morning after sex.
You do not study my form
in a low-cut tank
snatched out of the welfare bin
at church
where we half-attend for charity
and free Sunday casseroles—
macaroni and Velveeta cheese.
You never ask me for sex in the morning
or leave an ice cube in your glass
for me to suck

and crush between my teeth.
And you never drink anything
you wouldn't want me to drink
in private, at home.
And you are never at home,
often gone before I wake.
You leave early,
never tired,
adapted to the rhythm of my churning
all night
on the opposite side of a mattress—
like this wingless fly
basking in the sun
on a windowsill.
I poke at its black bulb to see if it
could kick.

// EX POST FACTO:
Repent

After
he held her under

his moist chest, mouth, waves
of ash-blond hair,

          She said

I'm sorry—

        She didn't mean to drown her cheeks.
        She didn't mean

to wake up, swim to the surface,
gasp
so wildly for air.

        His subtle accusations

        acquitted early morning,
        their consensus

        to stifle the past,
though they would repeat it again.

Notes

Commentary on Leviticus taken from *Matthew Henry's Commentary on the Whole Bible: Volume I – Genesis to Exodus* by Matthew Henry, Devoted Publishing; 1st edition, 2017.

"Open closed open. That's all we are." is from Yehuda Amichai's poem "Open Closed Open."

The concept of "body memories" is theoretical, espousing that the body, like the brain, is capable of storing memory in its tissues. Body memories are commonly referred to as part of the experience of PTSD. (see *Trauma and Memory* by Dr. Peter A. Levine & *The Body Keeps the Score: Brain, Mind, and Body in the Healing of Trauma* by Bessel van der Kolk, M. D.)

Thank You

Editors, readers, and designers at Sundress Publications for finding value in this manuscript and helping me bring it together in this final form. I deeply appreciate the work Erin Elizabeth Smith and the volunteer staff do to support survivors of assault and the stories we need to tell.

New England College (NEC) and the MFA program there for nurturing the majority of these poems as well as my emotional life as I worked through them, and specifically my MFA mentor Paige Ackerson-Kiely for her dedicated feedback on these poems.

Dennis Hinrichsen, who enthusiastically helped me revise some of these poems and draft a first manuscript. Without Dennis, I would know little about putting together a book-length project.

To my many cheerleaders who have encouraged my voice and bravery, specifically Jeffrey Bean, Robert Fanning, Denise Acevedo, Julie L. Moore, Phil Goldstein, Luke Johnson, TJ Chamberlin, Genevieve Pfeiffer, Dan Davis, and Sara Paye. I am deeply grateful for all of the support and encouragement I have received from each of these individuals over the last decade as I have engaged intuitive narrative therapy and research concerning the physical, psychological, and emotional impact of childhood sexual trauma on a victim's entire life, as well as the lived realities of domestic violence.

Dailey and Ryley Priest, my two children, who have listened to some of these poems and survived these experiences with me—and who brag about me to family and friends because I am a successful poet. Without you both, I may not be here today, still breathing and leveraging hope. You are brave, intelligent, and resourceful souls who teach me value each day. I love you.

About the Author

Kimberly Ann Priest is the author of three chapbooks, *Parrot Flower* from Glass Poetry Press, *still life* from PANK Press as a finalist for their Little Book Awards, and *White Goat Black Sheep* from Finishing Line Press. She is an MFA graduate in Creative Writing from New England College, already holding an MA in English Language & Literature from Central Michigan University. A proud Michigan native, she has taught composition and creative writing courses for Michigan State University, Central Michigan University, and Alma College, and participated in local initiatives to increase awareness concerning sexual assault, survivorship, and healing through artistic expression.

Her writing carefully observes the intersections of gender violence, narrative identities, embodiment, trauma, and environmental issues as well as survival, wildness, joy & grief. Her poetry has appeared in literary journals such as *North Dakota Quarterly*, *Salamander*, *Borderlands*, *RELIEF*, *RiverSedge*, *The Meadow*, *Ruminate Magazine*, and *The Berkeley Poetry Review*. She has received several Pushcart

Prize nominations and is a winner of the 2019 Heartland Poetry Prize in *New Poetry from the Midwest*, an annual anthology by New American Press. Currently, she teaches as an Assistant Professor of First-Year Writing at Michigan State University, is an associate poetry editor for the *Nimrod International Journal of Prose and Poetry* and Embody Reader for *The Maine Review*. Find more of her work at kimberlyannpriest.com.

Other Sundress Titles

Dad Jokes from Late in the Patriarchy
Amorak Huey
$16

What Nothing
Anna Meister
$16

Hood Criatura
féi hernandez
$16

Maps of Injury
Chera Hammons
$16

Lessons in Breathing Underwater
H.K. Hummel
$16

Dead Man's Float
Ruth Foley
$16

Blood Stripes
Aaron Graham
$16

Arabilis
Leah Silvieus
$16

Match Cut
Letitia Trent
$16

The Valley
Esteban Rodriguez
$16

To Everything There Is
Donna Vorreyer
$16

nightsong
Ever Jones
$16

JAW
Albert Abonado
$16

Bury Me in Thunder
syan jay
$16

Gender Flytrap
Zoë Estelle Hitzel
$16

Boom Box
Amorak Huey
$16

Afakasi | Half-Caste
Hali F. Sofala-Jones
$16

Marvels
MR Sheffield
$20

CPSIA information can be obtained
at www.ICGtesting.com
Printed in the USA
JSHW040208230621
16111JS00004B/18